A BUSINESS APPROACH TO WATERMELON FARMING

I0429999

Complete Entrepreneurial Step By Step Guide To Watermelon Garden From Scratch

ZHURI HART

DISCLAIMER

This book is intended to provide general information and insights on adopting a business approach to farming. The content within is based on the author's knowledge and experiences up to the date of publication. It is essential to recognize that the field of agriculture is dynamic, influenced by various factors such as market conditions, climate, and regulatory changes.

Readers are advised to conduct thorough research, seek professional advice, and consider their unique circumstances before implementing any strategies or practices discussed in this book. The author and publisher disclaim any responsibility for the accuracy, completeness, or suitability of the information provided. The book is not a substitute for professional advice, and the author and publisher shall not be liable for any damages or losses arising from the use or reliance on the information presented herein.

Individual results may vary, and success in farming enterprises is contingent upon numerous variables. The author encourages readers to consult with relevant experts, agricultural extension services, and legal or financial professionals to tailor strategies to their specific needs and local conditions.

This book is not intended to be a comprehensive guide to all aspects of farming, and readers should exercise their judgment and discretion in applying the principles discussed. The author and publisher do not endorse any specific products, services, or companies mentioned in this book unless explicitly stated.

By reading this book, the reader acknowledges and accepts the inherent uncertainties in agricultural endeavors and agrees to use the information at their own risk.

TABLE OF CONTENTS

CHAPTER ONE 11

WATERMELON FARMING INTRODUCTION 11

KNOWING HOW TO FARM WATERMELON 11

AN OVERVIEW OF GROWING WATERMELON 11

WATERMELON VARIETIES 12

CONDITIONS OF THE SOIL AND CLIMATE........................12

TECHNIQUES FOR WATERING AND IRRIGATION 13

CHAPTER TWO 15

ORGANIZING YOUR FARM TO GROW WATERMELON...........15

ESTABLISHING OBJECTIVES AND GOALS 15

FORMULATING A BUSINESS STRATEGY...........................15

SELECTING A SITE AND PREPARING THE LAND 16

TOOLS AND EQUIPMENT...17

CHAPTER THREE 19

SELECTION AND GERMINATION OF SEEDS........................19

SELECTION OF SEEDS IS CRUCIAL 19

POPULAR TYPES OF WATERMELONS 19

METHODS FOR GERMINATION OF SEEDS 20

NURSERY ADMINISTRATION 21

CHAPTER FOUR 23

PLANTING AND MANAGING CROPS 23

PLANTING SEEDLINGS 23

PLANTING AND SPACING SCHEMES 23

REMOVING WEEDS AND MULCHING 24

METHODS OF FERTILIZATION 25

CHAPTER FIVE...27

CONTROL OF PESTS AND DISEASES IN WATERMELON 27

TYPICAL PESTS IN THE FARMING OF WATERMELON 27

WATERMELON-RELATED DISEASES................................27

STRATEGIES FOR INTEGRATED PEST MANAGEMENT (IPM) 28

CHAPTER SIX...31

HARVESTING WATERMELON AND MANAGING IT AFTER HARVEST.......31

ASSESSING RIPENESS...31

METHODS OF HARVESTING..32

POST-HARVEST STORAGE AND HANDLING 32

MEASURES FOR QUALITY CONTROL..............................33

CHAPTER SEVEN 35

MARKETING STRATEGIES FOR WATERMELON FARMERS.......................35

MARKET ANALYSIS 35

PACKAGING & BRANDING 35

DISTRIBUTION CHANNELS 36

STRATEGIES FOR PRICING 37

CHAPTER EIGHT...39

MANAGING MONEY IN WATERMELON AGRICULTURE 39

COST ESTIMATION..39

PLANNING AND BUDGETING.......................................40

RISK CONTROL...41

ABOUT THE BOOK

For those looking to start and grow their watermelon farming businesses, the book "A Business Approach to Watermelon Farming" is an invaluable reference. The Introduction portion of this extensive guide gives readers a foundation on the importance of watermelon growing in the agricultural landscape through a thorough investigation.

The book's goal is made apparent, with a focus on providing new and seasoned farmers with the knowledge and abilities they need. The content is tailored to suit a diverse readership, ranging from novices to experienced professionals, thanks to the clear definition of the scope and audience.

A thorough examination of the principles of watermelon production is started, which also provides information on cultivars, soil and climate requirements, and irrigation methods. This background information establishes the framework for the next chapters and provides readers with a solid basis upon which to build.

By emphasizing the strategic planning involved in watermelon farming, from goal-setting and business planning to site selection and equipment concerns, the book lifts the conversation. This section offers farmers a road map for successfully optimizing their operations.

It goes into great detail about the crucial part that seed selection and germination play in the cultivation process. This chapter walks readers through common watermelon kinds and germination methods in addition to educating them on the significance of seed selection. The practical components of planting and crop management are covered in detail, which includes subjects like fertilization techniques, transplanting, and spacing. Gaining these insights is essential to guaranteeing crop health and maximum output.

Integrated pest management solutions are introduced and common challenges are explored, with a focus on watermelon pest and disease management. which covers post-harvest handling, quality control procedures, and harvesting techniques, becomes increasingly important as the growing process advances. The book shift to the business side of watermelon farming, delving into financial management and marketing tactics, offering a comprehensive perspective of the farming operation.

An engaging section that includes case studies and success stories brings the book to a close. Through these in-depth accounts of prosperous watermelon farms, readers can gain practical examples, best practices, and perspectives. All things considered, "A Business Approach to Watermelon Farming" is a thorough and useful manual that acts as a guide for anyone navigating the complex terrain of watermelon farming.

CHAPTER ONE

WATERMELON FARMING
INTRODUCTION

KNOWING HOW TO FARM WATERMELON

Watermelon farming is an important aspect of agriculture that is practiced in many parts of the world since watermelons are a popular and nutritious fruit. This type of agriculture requires a thorough awareness of several variables, from irrigation methods to soil and climate conditions. In this overview, we explore the key ideas that influence the field of watermelon cultivation.

AN OVERVIEW OF GROWING WATERMELON

The overview of watermelon agriculture summarizes the various steps that go into producing this fruit. Citrullus lanatus, the scientific name for watermelons, is a member of the Cucurbitaceae family. To produce a satisfactory harvest, watermelon growing involves careful planning and attention to agricultural principles.

To maximize yields, farmers carry out procedures including seed selection, land preparation, planting, and post-harvest management.

WATERMELON VARIETIES

There are many different types of watermelons, and each one is identified by its attributes like size, shape, color, and flavor. The kind of soil, market demand, and climate all influence the choice of watermelon cultivar. Traditional red-fleshed watermelons, seedless watermelons, yellow-fleshed watermelons, and miniature or personal-sized watermelons are common variations. Choosing the right variety is essential to satisfying market trends and customer preferences.

CONDITIONS OF THE SOIL AND CLIMATE

A key factor in the success of watermelon farming is the soil's requirements and climate. Warm weather is ideal for watermelons, and elements like sunlight, humidity, and frost sensitivity affect their growth. Fertility and well-draining soils are necessary for the best possible watermelon production. To evaluate if their soil needs to be amended with nutrients and organic matter, farmers frequently examine the composition and structure of the soil.

TECHNIQUES FOR WATERING AND IRRIGATION

Water is a major factor in crop health and productivity, thus watering and irrigation strategies are an essential part of growing watermelon. The watermelon plant needs a well-regulated irrigation system because it has different moisture requirements at different phases of growth. To effectively feed water to the plants, farmers use drip irrigation, furrow irrigation, and sprinkler irrigation. With careful watering, problems like fruit cracking can be avoided and watermelons that are delicious and succulent will grow.

Growing watermelon requires a comprehensive strategy that includes several aspects, such as managing soil and climate conditions, choosing appropriate kinds, and comprehending the subtleties of culture. Watermelon crops depend on farmers to maintain their development and productivity through the use of efficient irrigation methods and the adoption of optimum agricultural practices. For individuals who are new to watermelon farming as well as experienced growers, this introduction lays the groundwork for a deeper examination of each idea and clarifies the nuances of the industry.

CHAPTER TWO

ORGANIZING YOUR FARM TO GROW WATERMELON

ESTABLISHING OBJECTIVES AND GOALS

Planning your watermelon farm starts with defining your goals and objectives. Start by outlining your goals for the farm, such as creating a successful business, supplying regional markets, or supporting community agriculture. Your objectives ought to be SMART— specific, measurable, realistic, relevant, and time-bound. Take into account variables including your farm's size, anticipated production, and financial goals. Your objectives will serve as a guide for decision-making and resource allocation during the planning phase if they are stated clearly.

FORMULATING A BUSINESS STRATEGY

Making a thorough business strategy is crucial to your watermelon farm's success. Your objective, vision, and values should all be outlined in this paper, along with the tactics you'll use to get there. Provide a thorough market study that takes into account variables including pricing, competition, and demand. Your company strategy should also include a contingency plan, risk management techniques, and financial estimates. In addition to providing direction, a well-written business plan is an invaluable resource for securing funding or forming alliances.

SELECTING A SITE AND PREPARING THE LAND

The preparation of the soil and the choice of site are essential components in watermelon farm planning. Select a site where the soil is in good condition, taking drainage, fertility, and texture into account. Well-drained sandy loam soils with a pH of slightly acidic to neutral are ideal for watermelons. Proper exposure to sunshine is crucial, so pick a spot that receives enough of it. Think about accessibility for transit and closeness to water supplies for irrigation. After the place has been chosen, concentrate on preparing the ground by removing any debris, plowing the area, and adding organic materials. A solid base of prepared ground is essential for producing good watermelon crops.

TOOLS AND EQUIPMENT

Choosing the appropriate tools and equipment is essential for productive and successful farm operations. Take into account the size of your watermelon farm and make equipment purchases that will help you reach your production targets.

For preparing the ground, tractors, plows, and cultivators are necessary, and drip irrigation systems can maximize water use. Your operation's size should determine the harvesting instruments you choose, such as knives and pruning shears. Equipment lifetime and reliable operation depend heavily on routine maintenance and repair. By matching the appropriate equipment to your watermelon farm's unique requirements, you may cut labor expenses and increase productivity.

Effective planning for a watermelon farm includes establishing specific goals and objectives, creating a thorough business plan, picking a site with care, and properly preparing the ground. Having the appropriate tools and equipment on your farm guarantees smooth operations. By taking care of these important ideas, you lay the groundwork for a successful watermelon farming enterprise.

CHAPTER THREE

SELECTION AND GERMINATION OF SEEDS

SELECTION OF SEEDS IS CRUCIAL

A crop's performance is largely dependent on the selection of seeds, which is an essential stage in the cultivation process. The capacity of seed selection to affect several variables, including yield, disease resistance, and general plant vigor, makes it crucial. When choosing seeds, farmers and gardeners need to take into account things like climate, type of soil, and intended usage. Furthermore, characteristics like resilience to pests, drought, and local conditions adaptation are critical for guaranteeing a robust and fruitful crop.

POPULAR TYPES OF WATERMELONS

A popular and extensively consumed fruit, watermelon comes in many different types, each with its unique qualities. Popular watermelon types include the Jubilee, which is prized for its huge size and sweet taste, the Sugar Baby, which is a smaller variety ideal for smaller gardens, and the Crimson Sweet, which is recognized for its crisp and sweet flesh. Because every variety has its characteristics, farmers must choose seeds that suit their requirements as well as the conditions of their environment.

METHODS FOR GERMINATION OF SEEDS

Techniques for seed germination are essential to starting a new plant from a seed. This procedure entails creating the ideal environment—one that includes warmth, moisture, and oxygen—for the seed embryo to begin maturing into a seedling.

Direct sowing, in which seeds are sown directly in the ground, and pre-germination, in which seeds are soaked or given additional treatments before planting, are common germination strategies. Optimizing the germination process requires an understanding of the germination requirements of individual plants.

NURSERY ADMINISTRATION

A crucial component of productive crop development, particularly when beginning with seeds, is nursery management. Establishing a setting that supports seedling development is a key component of good nursery management. During this phase, it is critical to have elements like proper watering, sufficient light, and temperature regulation.

Additionally, maintaining the health and vitality of seedlings is greatly influenced by disease prevention and pest control. Because a well-managed nursery gives plants a solid basis to grow before they are transplanted into the field, it contributes to the crop's overall success.

The importance of seed selection cannot be emphasized because it directly affects how the entire cultivation process turns out. With so many different types of watermelon to choose from, producers can select seeds that suit their tastes and regional climate. The effective transfer from seed to robust, healthy plants depends on subsequent procedures like nursery management and seed germination techniques, which demand meticulous attention to detail. All things considered, a knowledgeable approach to these ideas is necessary to attain the best possible crop cultivation outcomes.

CHAPTER FOUR

PLANTING AND MANAGING CROPS

PLANTING SEEDLINGS

A critical phase in the cultivation procedure that's frequently used to guarantee ideal plant growth and development is transplanting seedlings. To continue their maturation, young plants are moved from their original germination or nursery area to a specified field or garden. Usually, the purpose of transplanting is to provide seedlings with more room, better soil, and an environment that suits their requirements. For plants that are sensitive to crowded circumstances in their early growth phases, this procedure is especially crucial.

PLANTING AND SPACING SCHEMES

Crop yield and general health are greatly influenced by planting and spacing practices. The way that plants are arranged in a field or garden greatly influences how easily they can receive water, nutrients, and sunlight. Overcrowding can result in competition for resources and greater vulnerability to diseases, therefore proper spacing is crucial to preventing this. Planting patterns, including row spacing and plant arrangement, are thoughtfully planned to maximize the use of available resources and space, guaranteeing that every plant has enough area to grow and prosper.

REMOVING WEEDS AND MULCHING

Mulching is a basic crop management practice where a layer of either organic or inorganic material is applied to the soil surrounding plants. This barrier has several functions, such as controlling temperature, retaining moisture, and suppressing weeds. Mulching creates a barrier that prevents undesirable plants from emerging, moderates temperature variations in the soil, and helps preserve soil moisture by minimizing evaporation. Mulch also adds organic matter to the soil through its slow decomposition, which improves soil fertility.

A key part of crop management is weed control, which reduces the competition that weeds and crops have for vital resources. Weeds can reduce agricultural production by posing a competition for sunlight, water, and nutrients. Effective weed control involves a variety of techniques, such as hand-pulling weeds, mulching, and using herbicides. In addition to these techniques, crop rotation, and cover crops also help reduce weeds by upsetting the life cycle of some weed species and enhancing soil health in general.

METHODS OF FERTILIZATION

Fertilization techniques are essential for giving crops the nutrients they need for healthy growth and yield. To treat nutrient deficits that can restrict plant development, fertilizers are added to the soil to increase or supplement its existing nutrient content. Choosing the right fertilizers, applying them at the right times, and applying them at the right rates are important factors in creating a successful fertilization plan.

Proper root development, strong plant growth, and the yield of nutrient-dense, high-quality crops all depend on balanced nutrient levels. Sustainable fertilizing techniques limit any effects on ecosystems and water quality by taking environmental factors into account.

CHAPTER FIVE

CONTROL OF PESTS AND DISEASES IN WATERMELON

TYPICAL PESTS IN THE FARMING OF WATERMELON

Pests that affect watermelon cultivation can have a big impact on crop quality and productivity. Aphids are widespread pests that feed on the sap of watermelon plants, resulting in restricted development and virus transmission. Cucumber beetles are another noteworthy pest; in addition to feeding on leaves, they can spread bacterial wilt, which causes plants to wilt and eventually die. Furthermore, crops of watermelon may become infested by spider mites and whiteflies, which can cause damage by eating the plants and spreading disease.

WATERMELON-RELATED DISEASES

A variety of diseases can affect watermelon plants, jeopardizing both their well-being and yield. Fusarium wilt, which is brought on by the soil-borne fungus Fusarium oxysporum, is one common illness. This illness may cause the plant to eventually wilt, have yellowing leaves, and die. The fungus Colletotrichum orbicular is the source of anthracnose, a frequent disease of watermelon that causes dark lesions on the fruit and leaves. Another major problem is powdery mildew, which causes a white, powdery substance to accumulate on leaves, impeding photosynthesis and decreasing output.

STRATEGIES FOR INTEGRATED PEST MANAGEMENT (IPM)

In watermelon farming, integrated pest management (IPM) is a comprehensive approach that prioritizes ecologically responsible and sustainable methods for controlling pests and illnesses. A key component of integrated pest management (IPM) is crop rotation, which modifies the host plant to interfere with the life cycle of pests and diseases. To manage pest populations, biological control also entails the introduction of natural predators like nematodes or beneficial insects. This lessens the need for chemical pesticides and contributes to the ecosystem's continued equilibrium.

IPM heavily relies on cultural practices, such as planting plants at the right distance apart to improve air circulation and lower disease risk. Mulching is another useful tactic since it helps keep weeds under control that could be home to illnesses and pests. Additionally, choosing watermelon cultivars that are resistant to illnesses is a proactive approach to integrated pest management (IPM) since these varieties can resist specific pests and diseases, reducing the need for chemical interventions.

Chemical control in integrated pest management (IPM) refers to the prudent use of pesticides when pest populations surpass predetermined thresholds, yet with moderation.

To reduce the impact on ecosystem components and beneficial creatures, however, this strategy places a higher priority on the use of less hazardous and ecologically friendly chemicals.

A thorough strategy that incorporates a variety of tactics is needed for the efficient management of watermelon pests and diseases. Incorporating Integrated Pest Management (IPM) techniques not only shields the crop from pests and illnesses but also fosters sustainability and long-term profitability in the watermelon industry.

CHAPTER SIX
HARVESTING WATERMELON AND MANAGING IT AFTER HARVEST

ASSESSING RIPENESS

The first step in harvesting watermelon is to assess the fruit's ideal level of maturity. To guarantee that the fruit is at its best in terms of flavor and nutrients, ripeness must be determined. Ripeness can be determined using several indications, including color, texture, and sound.

Finding the "ground spot," or creamy yellow mark on the underside that denotes the fruit has matured on the vine, is the conventional approach. Ripeness is also indicated by a deep, hollow sound produced when tapping the skin and by a dull feel.

Together, these audible and visual clues help farmers choose watermelons that are ready to be harvested.

METHODS OF HARVESTING

Watermelons must be harvested carefully to prevent harm and maintain quality. Hand harvesting is a popular technique in which knowledgeable workers cut the fruit from the vine, leaving a short stem intact, using knives or shears. Throughout this process, you must handle the watermelons carefully to avoid any bruises or cracks. Larger-scale enterprises also use mechanical harvesting, which involves cutting and lifting the fruits with specialized equipment. To prevent harming the watermelons, this technique necessitates accuracy. Regardless of the method, picking fruit as soon as possible is essential to preventing overripening and guaranteeing it is in prime shape when it is sold.

POST-HARVEST STORAGE AND HANDLING

Ensuring that watermelons are properly stored and transported after harvesting is crucial to preserving their freshness. Cleaning the collected fruits to get rid of dirt and debris is the first step.

The watermelons are then cured, which lowers the chance of rot by enabling the sliced stem to mend. During storage, proper ventilation and temperature control are essential. Watermelons should ideally be stored at 50°F (10°C) or below to slow down the ripening process. To prevent moisture-related problems, the storage facility should have adequate humidity control and employ suitable stacking procedures to minimize damage.

MEASURES FOR QUALITY CONTROL

A crucial part of producing watermelons is quality control, which includes several steps to guarantee that the final product fulfills consumer expectations. Inspection procedures take place in a variety of settings, including the field, storage, and transit. To weed out spoiled or subpar fruits, inspectors evaluate characteristics like size, shape, color, and overall look. Quality control procedures may also involve the use of technology, such as handheld refractometers for measuring sugar content, in addition to visual inspections. By putting in place a strong quality control system, a watermelon company can preserve its reputation while guaranteeing that customers will always receive a high-quality product. Watermelon harvesting and post-harvest handling procedures are more successful overall when regular monitoring and adherence to industry standards are implemented.

CHAPTER SEVEN

MARKETING STRATEGIES FOR WATERMELON FARMERS

MARKET ANALYSIS

To grasp the workings of the industry and spot prospects, watermelon farmers must perform a thorough market analysis. Variations in geographical patterns of consumption as well as seasonal variations in demand should all be considered in the study. Farmers should also take into account consumer attitudes toward wellness and health, rivals' business plans, and market movements. Watermelon growers can become more competitive by customizing their production and marketing strategies to match certain consumer demands by gathering market knowledge.

PACKAGING & BRANDING

To differentiate themselves from competitors and win over customers, watermelon growers must establish a distinctive brand identity. This entails creating a distinctive brand identity, logo, and messaging that appeals to the intended market. Furthermore, spending money on useful and appealing packaging can have a big impact on product appeal and brand visibility. Growers want to think about packing solutions that not only preserve the watermelons' quality and freshness but also project dependability and professionalism.

Using environmentally friendly packaging options can also be in line with the growing sustainability aspirations of consumers.

DISTRIBUTION CHANNELS

Selecting the appropriate distribution channels is essential to guaranteeing that watermelons are delivered to customers effectively and in top shape. Farmers that grow watermelons can investigate a range of distribution channels, such as regional farmers' markets, supermarkets, grocers, and internet sites. Their product reach can be increased by working with nearby retailers and building connections with distributors. In addition, taking part in neighborhood gatherings and forming alliances with eateries and caterers might open up new distribution channels. Producers of watermelon can reduce the risks associated with relying on a single outlet by expanding their distribution network.

STRATEGIES FOR PRICING

Achieving the ideal pricing plan requires striking a careful balance between increasing earnings and maintaining market competitiveness. Farmers who grow watermelons should think about things like production costs, consumer demand, and the product's perceived worth.

Seasonal changes can also affect prices, necessitating adjustments to account for shifts in supply and demand. While premium pricing for specialist or organic types can cater to a particular market, offering promotions or discounts during high seasons can assist boost sales.

It is imperative to consistently assess pricing strategies in light of consumer feedback and market developments to maintain competitiveness and guarantee long-term profitability.

Watermelon growers can achieve success in their marketing endeavors by carrying out an exhaustive market analysis, crafting a robust brand identity, streamlining distribution routes, and executing impactful pricing tactics. Watermelon growers may position themselves for success in the cutthroat agriculture sector by knowing their customers' tastes, following market trends, and reacting to shifting circumstances.

CHAPTER EIGHT

MANAGING MONEY IN WATERMELON AGRICULTURE

COST ESTIMATION

Since it entails figuring out the costs related to different parts of the farming process, cost estimation is essential to the financial management of watermelon farming. This covers expenses for personnel, equipment, land preparation, seed procurement, irrigation systems, fertilizers, herbicides, and other running costs. Watermelon growers can deploy resources more effectively and decide on production methods with knowledge thanks to accurate cost estimation. The process of estimating costs is influenced by various factors, including the size of the farming enterprise, geographic location, and state of the market. Farmers are better able to sustain their financial stability and market competitiveness when cost estimates are routinely reviewed and adjusted.

Predicting the amount of money that will be made from the sale of watermelons is known as revenue forecasting in the watermelon farming industry. When estimating revenue, farmers must take into account variables including crop yield, pricing patterns, and market demand. Farmers are better equipped to identify development prospects, make wise investment decisions, and set realistic financial goals when revenue forecasting is done accurately. Creating accurate revenue estimates also requires an awareness of market dynamics and seasonal changes. Watermelon growers can improve the precision of their revenue forecasts by using market knowledge and historical data, which will ultimately lead to improved financial management and sustainable business practices.

PLANNING AND BUDGETING

To effectively manage finances in the watermelon growing industry, planning and budgeting are essential. Farmers can allocate resources more effectively and guarantee that expenses match revenue projections by following a well-structured budget. It entails putting together a thorough strategy for all financial components, such as capital expenditures, operating costs, production costs, and reserve funds. Financial planning encompasses long-term strategies for growth and sustainability, going beyond the current growing season. Watermelon farmers can avoid financial difficulties, take advantage of growth opportunities, and build a strong basis for financial success in the agricultural industry by carefully arranging their budgets and finances.

RISK CONTROL

Given the uncertainties involved in agriculture, risk management is an essential component of financial management in the watermelon industry. Several hazards, including unfavorable weather, pest infestations, unstable markets, and changes in input prices, can affect the financial performance of watermelon farms. Farmers must put risk-reduction plans into action, such as crop diversification, insurance, and the use of resilient agricultural techniques. To protect their financial interests, producers can make well-informed decisions by evaluating and comprehending the hazards unique to watermelon production. Farmers can improve the overall stability and resilience of their operations, reducing the possibility of financial failures and guaranteeing the industry's long-term success, by taking proactive measures to manage risks.

www.ingramcontent.com/pod-product-compliance
Lightning Source LLC
Chambersburg PA
CBHW070843290526
45795CB00002B/969